SRA
Research Projects

- Provides activities based on science and social studies content
- Helps students plan projects and conduct information searches
- Teaches the research process using varied resources

A Division of The McGraw·Hill Companies

Columbus, Ohio

www.sra4kids.com

SRA/McGraw-Hill

A Division of The **McGraw·Hill** *Companies*

Copyright © 2002 by SRA/McGraw-Hill.

All rights reserved. Except as permitted under the United States Copyright Act, no part of this publication may be reproduced or distributed in any form or by any means, or stored in a database or retrieval system, without the prior written permission of the publisher, unless otherwise indicated.

Send all inquiries to:
SRA/McGraw-Hill
8787 Orion Place
Columbus, OH 43240-4027

Printed in the United States of America.

ISBN 0-07-572382-4

    3 4 5 6 7 8 9 IPC 06 05 04

Table of Contents

Introduction

What Is the Program?

SRA Research Projects contains projects that can be used to extend and reinforce the skills your students are acquiring as they progress through *Reading Mastery Plus*. The projects are designed to be used with SRA/McGraw-Hill's *Research Assistant Software*, included in this booklet. The projects, designed to help develop student research skills, cover a range of content areas, including science, social studies, and geography.

How Does the Program Work?

This program provides five optional group research projects, all of which have blackline masters to help students organize information and evaluate their presentations. Each project is used to build upon an idea or information discussed in a lesson from the student textbook for *Reading Mastery Plus*. The projects connect to the ideas, information, or themes presented in those specified lessons. Projects are designed to be introduced after the lesson designated on the teacher directions has been completed. Each project specifies the content area being explored and states the objective.

To use the program:

- Select the projects you wish to present and schedule them at a time when the students have completed the targeted lessons in *Reading Mastery Plus*.

- Schedule sufficient time for each project. These projects are separated into four to six sessions. The projects can be completed in one week or several weeks depending on what your schedule allows.

- Direct students to utilize the *Research Assistant Software*. This software is vital to helping students develop their research skills and prepare their final presentations. Students should have access to the software throughout the time they are working on their projects. The teacher directions will give you suggestions of forms from the software that might be helpful to students in gathering and organizing data and in preparing their end-of-project presentations. A user's manual for the *Research Assistant* can be found at the back of this booklet. In addition to a description of the software capabilities, the manual also provides a description of each of the forms included on the software.

- The blackline masters are used to help keep the students on task and aid in the development of their research skills. The blackline masters should be copied for distribution to the groups. The answers to the blackline masters are included in the teacher directions.

- Each project includes a list of suggested resources. Some of these resources include books, magazines, newspapers, interviews, and the Internet. The variety of resources is designed to provide students with unique perspectives on the topics they are researching. The Internet could be a valuable resource. Refer to your school's Internet policy before allowing students access to the Internet. Your librarian or media center director can recommend many resources.

- Give students feedback as they work on the projects. The checkpoints found throughout the teacher directions provide opportunities for you to check each student's or group's progress and to help keep them on task.

- Evaluate student presentations by referring to the Evaluation/Answers section in the teacher directions.

Project 1 How Does Your Garden Grow?

TOPIC

Art, Science, Reading

Suggested Resources:

Blackline Masters 1, 2, and 3; Research Assistant Software; seed packets; garden catalogs; gardening articles from magazines and newspapers; pictures of plants; the Internet

Objective:

We use plants in many parts of our lives. We use them as food, as medicine, to repel insects, and as decoration. Using a variety of resources, find out about different types of plants and their characteristics. Use what you learn to invent a new type of plant and a seed packet for that plant.

Suggested Activities:

Session One

Divide students into groups of at least three members each and pass out Blackline Master 1 to help describe the project to the students.

Have each group obtain a Project Startup form. The Project Startup form can be found on the Research Assistant Software. Each group should complete the Project Startup form with the required information and turn it in to the teacher.

Direct each group to obtain and complete a Tasks form from the Research Assistant Software.

Once tasks have been assigned, provide students with the location of other forms on the Research Assistant Software that might assist them in the organization of their individual tasks.

Introduce several of the suggested resources that the students should use to research plants and develop their own plant. Allow time in class for groups to begin their research.

———————————————— CHECKPOINT ————————————————

Review the Project Startup form and Tasks form for each group; each student in the group should have an assignment.

Session Two

Allow time for students to use as many of the suggested resources as possible to complete the questions on Blackline Master 2. Encourage students to share information discovered with the class while reviewing the questions on the Blackline Master.

Possible answers for Blackline Master 2:
1. Roots, leaf, stem, flower, fruit, bulb
2. Source of food, medicine, beauty, repel certain insects, dye
3. All answers are acceptable.

Using resources from the suggested materials list and any other resources available, have students complete Blackline Master 3. After students have completed the Blackline Master, discuss the possible answers in class.

Possible answers for Blackline Master 3:
1. Any are acceptable if the student can show where the information was found on the seed packet.
2. Accept all reasonable answers.

Have each team obtain the Main Topic & Details form from the Research Assistant Software. Encourage them to use this form for organizing their information for the final product—a seed packet design for their created plant.

Allow time for students to invent a new plant based on their research of various types of plants.

─────────────── **CHECKPOINT** ───────────────

Review the Main Topic and Details form for each group to ensure that each group has invented its new type of plant.

Session Three

Have each group obtain a copy of the Notes form found in the Research Assistant Software to organize its ideas. Direct students to the Sources form found in the Research Assistant Software. This form may also help them organize their information.

Students should continue to look for information to include in their presentations.

─────────────── **CHECKPOINT** ───────────────

Require groups to turn in their Notes forms with, at least, the name of their creation at the bottom of the form. Check with individual students on their progress.

Session Four

Have each group obtain a copy of the Supplies form found in the Research Assistant Software. The Supplies form should be completed by the end of today's project time. Encourage students to share with you and other groups any supplies needed for their presentations.

Review with students the type of information found on a seed packet.

Allow time for groups to further develop their final presentations.

At the end of today's project time, ask each group to share with you any difficulties it may be experiencing regarding its presentation. If time allows, open the discussion to the entire class for classmates to offer suggestions and additional resources.

——————————————————— CHECKPOINT ———————————————————

Students will be required to turn in a rough draft of either the front or the back of their seed packet design.

Session Five

Using all resources, notes, and materials available, students will complete the final design of the seed packet, front and back, for their newly created plant. Once all designs have been turned in, have students assist in "planting" their seed packets on a windowsill or bulletin board using the information found on the packet pertaining to seed spacing, height, etc.

Evaluation/Answers:

Creativity and participation are essential; however, the finished product should contain the information needed to display the packets per directions in Session Five.

Optional Discussion:

Have students complete the Work on Project form from the Research Assistant Software. Facilitate a discussion in which the students discuss their likes and dislikes pertaining to the project, as well as their opinions regarding the difficulties they had completing their tasks.

How Does Your Garden Grow?
Blackline Master 1

Objective:

We use plants in many parts of our lives. We use them as food, as medicine, to repel insects, and as decoration. Using a variety of resources, find out about different types of plants and their characteristics. Use what you learn to invent a new type of plant and a seed packet for that plant.

Resource List:

☐ Research Assistant Software

☐ seed packets

☐ garden catalogs

☐ gardening articles from magazines and newspapers

☐ pictures of plants

☐ the Internet

☐ _____

☐ _____

☐ _____

Copyright © SRA/McGraw-Hill. Permission is granted to reproduce this page for classroom use. **Project 1** **5**

How Does Your Garden Grow?
Blackline Master 2

1. List the parts of a plant:

   _____   _____

   _____   _____

   _____   _____

   _____   _____

2. List different ways that plants are used:

   _____

   _____

   _____

   _____

   _____

3. Use your imagination to think of new ways for plants to be used, and list
   them below:

   _____

   _____

   _____

   _____

   _____

   _____

   _____

    Copyright © SRA/McGraw-Hill. Permission is granted to reproduce this page for classroom use.

How Does Your Garden Grow?
Blackline Master 3

Look at a seed packet and answer the following questions:

1. What information is found on a seed packet?

_____

_____

_____

_____

_____

2. Why is *all* of the information important?

_____

_____

_____

_____

_____

Copyright © SRA/McGraw-Hill. Permission is granted to reproduce this page for classroom use.

Project 2   What's Bugging You?

TOPIC

*Art, Science,
Reading*

Suggested Resources:

Blackline Masters 1 and 2; Research Assistant Software; insect identification books; scientific magazines; interviews; the Internet

Objective:

Many insects experience several stages of life. Just as Herman began life as an egg, became a worm/maggot, then changed into a fly, other insects also go through life stages. Using a variety of resources, find out about other insects that experience several life stages. Use visual aids, such as models or cartoons, to show the life stages of the insect you have chosen to study and share what you have learned with your classmates.

Suggested Activities:

Session One

Divide students into groups of at least three members each and pass out Blackline Master 1 to help describe the project to the students.

Have each group obtain a Project Startup form. The Project Startup form can be found on the Research Assistant Software. Each group should complete the Project Startup form with the required information and turn it in to the teacher.

Direct each group to obtain and complete a Tasks form from the Research Assistant Software.

Once tasks have been assigned, provide students with the location of other forms on the Research Assistant Software that might assist them in the organization of their individual tasks.

Introduce several of the suggested resources that the students should use to research insects that experience different stages of life. Allow time in class for groups to begin their research.

———————————————— CHECKPOINT ————————————————

Review the Project Startup form and Tasks form for each group; each student in the group should have an assignment.

Session Two

Allow time for students to use as many of the suggested resources as possible to complete the questions on Blackline Master 2. Encourage students to share information discovered with the class while reviewing the questions on the Blackline Master.

Possible answers for Blackline Master 2:
1. flies, butterflies, moths, locusts, etc.
2. All reasonable answers are acceptable.

Direct each group to obtain and complete a Main Topic & Details form from the Research Assistant Software.

Allow time for students to choose which insect their presentations will cover.

———————————————— **CHECKPOINT** ————————————————

Review the Main Topic & Details form for each group to ensure that each group has chosen a specific insect.

Session Three

Have each group obtain a Supplies form found in the Research Assistant Software. The Supplies form should be completed by the end of today's project time. Encourage students to share with you and other groups any supplies needed for their presentations.

Allow time for groups to further develop their final presentations.

At the end of today's project time, ask each group to share with you any difficulties it may be experiencing regarding its presentation. If time allows, open the discussion to the entire class for classmates to offer suggestions and additional resources.

Session Four

Allow time for groups to work on their final presentations.

——————— **CHECKPOINT** ———————

At the end of today's project time, each group should have a presentation and visual aid prepared.

Session Five

Presentation of project including visual aid(s).

To further the students' understanding of the project, an art show or a zoo might be set up. Students could explain to small groups of students from other classrooms what they learned.

Evaluation/Answers:

Each presentation should include at least one visual aid that demonstrates an understanding of the different stages in the life of the chosen insect.

Optional Discussion:

Have students complete the Knowledge form from the Research Assistant Software. Facilitate a discussion in which the students discuss what they learned by doing the project and what they would still like to learn.

What's Bugging You?

Blackline Master 1

Objective:

Many insects experience several stages of life. Just as Herman began life as an egg, became a worm/maggot, then changed into a fly, other insects also go through life stages. Using a variety of resources, find out about other insects that experience several life stages. Use visual aids, such as models or cartoons, to show the life stages of the insect you have chosen to study and share what you have learned with your classmates.

Resource List:

☐ Research Assistant Software

☐ insect identification books

☐ magazine articles

☐ magazine or book pictures

☐ interviews with local experts such as an exterminator, a science teacher, a county extension or agriculture agent, or a university professor

☐ zoo

☐ the Internet

☐ _____

☐ _____

☐ _____

Copyright © SRA/McGraw-Hill. Permission is granted to reproduce this page for classroom use.

What's Bugging You?

Blackline Master 2

1. List some of the insects you have discovered that go through different life stages:

_____   _____

_____   _____

_____   _____

_____   _____

2. List some of the words you have found that describe these different stages:

_____

_____

_____

_____

_____

 Copyright © SRA/McGraw-Hill. Permission is granted to reproduce this page for classroom use.

Project 3   Weather Effects

Use after Lesson 42

TOPIC

Art, Science, Reading, Social Studies

Suggested Resources:

Blackline Masters 1 and 2; Research Assistant Software; weather maps; almanacs; interviews; the Internet

Objective:

Weather is an important part of our lives. It affects how we dress, when we participate in activities, and how and where we travel. Using a variety of resources, including weather maps and almanacs, find out about people whose work is affected daily by the weather. Develop a presentation about one of these people and the work he or she does. Use visual aids, such as weather maps, charts, and examples of protective equipment, to share what you have learned with your classmates.

Suggested Activities:

Session One

Divide students into groups of at least three members each and pass out Blackline Master 1 to help describe the project to the students.

Have each group obtain a Project Startup form. The Project Startup form can be found on the Research Assistant Software. Each group should complete the Project Startup form with the required information and turn it in to the teacher.

Direct each group to obtain and complete a Tasks form from the Research Assistant Software.

Once tasks have been assigned, provide students with the location of other forms on the Research Assistant Software that might assist them in the organization of their individual tasks.

Introduce several of the suggested resources that the students should use to research occupations affected by the weather and some of the activities of the occupations. Allow time in class for groups to begin their research.

———————————————— **CHECKPOINT** ————————————————

Review the Project Startup form and Tasks form for each group; each student in the group should have an assignment.

Session Two

Allow time for students to use as many of the suggested resources as possible to complete the questions on Blackline Master 2. Encourage students to share information discovered with the class while reviewing the questions on the Blackline Master.

Possible answers for Blackline Master 2:
1. All answers are acceptable. Some examples are pilots, construction workers, and landscapers.
2. All answers are acceptable.

Direct each group to obtain and complete a Main Topic & Details form from the Research Assistant Software.

Allow time for students to choose a person whose work they wish to research.

————————————————— **CHECKPOINT** —————————————————

Review the Main Topics & Details form for each group to ensure that each group has narrowed its research to one occupation.

Session Three

Have each group obtain a Supplies form found in the Research Assistant Software. The Supplies form should be completed by the end of today's project time. Encourage students to share with you and other groups any supplies needed for their presentations.

Allow time for groups to further develop their presentations.

At the end of today's project time, ask each group to share with you any difficulties it may be experiencing regarding its presentation. If time allows, open the discussion to the entire class for classmates to offer suggestions and additional resources.

Session Four

Allow time for groups to work on their final presentations.

—————————————— CHECKPOINT ——————————————

At the end of today's project time, each group should have a majority of its presentation and visual aid completed.

Session Five

Presentation of project including visual aid(s).

To further the students' understanding of the project, a "Job Fair" might be set up where students have a booth dedicated to the person and occupation they researched. Students could explain to small groups of students from other classrooms what they have learned.

Evaluation/Answers:

Each presentation should include at least one visual aid that conveys an understanding of how the weather affects the occupation.

Optional Discussion:

Have students complete the Work on Project form from the Research Assistant Software. Facilitate a discussion in which the students discuss their likes and dislikes pertaining to the project, as well as their opinions regarding the difficulties they had completing their tasks.

Weather Effects
Blackline Master 1

Objective:
Weather is an important part of our lives. It affects how we dress, when we participate in activities, and how and where we travel. Using a variety of resources, including weather maps and almanacs, find out about people whose work is affected daily by the weather. Develop a presentation about one of these people and the work he or she does. Use visual aids, such as weather maps, charts, and examples of protective equipment, to share what you have learned with your classmates.

Resource List:

☐ Research Assistant Software

☐ weather maps

☐ almanacs

☐ interviews with people whose work is affected daily by the weather

☐ the Internet

☐ _____

☐ _____

☐ _____

Copyright © SRA/McGraw-Hill. Permission is granted to reproduce this page for classroom use.

Weather Effects
Blackline Master 2

1. List three people whose work is affected daily by the weather:

   _____

   _____

   _____

2. List some of the activities each person has and how his or her activities might be changed according to the weather:

   _____

   _____

   _____

   _____

   _____

   _____

Copyright © SRA/McGraw-Hill. Permission is granted to reproduce this page for classroom use.

Project 4 Where in the United States?

Use after Lesson 48

TOPIC
Geography,
Reading,
Writing

Suggested Resources:
Blackline Masters 1, 2, and 3; Research Assistant Software; encyclopedia; atlas; maps; magazines; newspapers; geography book; globe; the Internet

Objective:
From the Atlantic to the Pacific, from Canada to Mexico, the United States of America is a colorful country, with a variety of landscapes and cultures. Using a variety of resources, find out about the geography, natural resources, and people of a state you have visited or would like to visit. Create a visual aid, such as a brochure or commercial, to help you share what you have learned with your classmates.

Suggested Activities:

Session One
Divide students into groups of at least three members each and pass out Blackline Master 1 to help describe the project to the students.

Have each group obtain a Project Startup form. The Project Startup form can be found on the Research Assistant Software. Each group should complete the Project Startup form with the required information and turn it in to the teacher.

Direct each group to obtain and complete a Tasks form from the Research Assistant Software.

Once tasks have been assigned, provide students with the location of other forms in the Research Assistant Software that might assist them in the organization of their individual tasks.

Ask if anyone has lived in or visited another part of the state or country. Allow students to share any of the differences they noticed during their stay.

Introduce several of the suggested resources that the students should use to research different states in the country. Allow time in class for groups to begin their research.

—————————————— CHECKPOINT ——————————————

Review the Project Startup form and Tasks form for each group; each student in the group should have an assignment.

Session Two

Allow time for students to use as many of the suggested resources as possible to complete the questions on Blackline Master 2. Encourage students to share information discovered with the class while reviewing the questions on the Blackline Master.

Possible answers for Blackline Master 2:
1. All are acceptable.
2. Anything other than "I just want to".
3. All are acceptable if they provide a lead to the final objective.

Direct each group to obtain and complete a Main Topic & Details form from the Research Assistant Software.

Direct each group to obtain and complete the Methods form found in the Research Assistant Software. This form will help groups choose the best method of presentation for their project. Tell students that it will be due at the next project session.

Allow time for students to choose a state they wish to research.

────────────────── CHECKPOINT ──────────────────

Review the Main Topic & Details form for each group to ensure that each group has narrowed its research to one state.

Session Three

Have each group obtain a Supplies form found in the Research Assistant Software. The Supplies form should be completed by the end of today's project time. Encourage students to share with you and other groups any supplies needed for their presentations.

Allow time for groups to further develop their presentations.

Have each group obtain a Sources form found in the Research Assistant Software. This form may help them organize their information.

At the end of today's project time, ask each group to share with you any difficulties it may be experiencing regarding its presentation. If time allows, open the discussion to the entire class for classmates to offer suggestions and additional resources.

Using resources from the suggested materials list and any other resources available, have students complete Blackline Master 3. After students have completed the Blackline Master, discuss the possible answers in class.

────────────────── CHECKPOINT ──────────────────

Review the Methods form for each group to ensure that each group has decided on a way to present their findings.

Session Four

Students should continue to research information for their presentation.

Allow time for groups to work on their final presentations.

——————————————— **CHECKPOINT** ———————————————

At the end of today's project time, each group should have a majority of its presentation and visual aid completed.

Session Five

Presentation of project including visual aid(s).

To further the students' understanding of the project, an art show or a travel fair might be set up. Students could explain to small groups of students from other classrooms what they have learned.

Evaluation/Answers:

Each presentation should include at least one visual aid that conveys an understanding of the geography, natural resources, and people of the chosen state.

Optional Discussion:

Have students complete the Work on Project form from the Research Assistant Software. Facilitate a discussion in which the students discuss their likes and dislikes pertaining to the project, as well as their opinions regarding the difficulties they had completing their tasks.

Where in the United States?

Blackline Master 1

Objective:

From the Atlantic to the Pacific, from Canada to Mexico, the United States of America is a colorful country, with a variety of landscapes and cultures. Using a variety of resources, find out about the geography, natural resources, and people of a state you have visited or would like to visit. Create a visual aid, such as a brochure or commercial, to help you share what you have learned with your classmates.

Resource List:

☐ Research Assistant Software

☐ encyclopedia

☐ atlas

☐ magazines

☐ newspapers

☐ geography book

☐ globe

☐ the Internet

☐ _____

☐ _____

☐ _____

Copyright © SRA/McGraw-Hill. Permission is granted to reproduce this page for classroom use.

Where in the United States?
Blackline Master 2

1. What state in the United States would you like to visit?

   _____

2. Why would you like to visit this place?

   _____

   _____

   _____

   _____

   _____

3. Where will you look for information about this place?

   _____

   _____

   _____

   _____

   _____

   _____

   Copyright © SRA/McGraw-Hill. Permission is granted to reproduce this page for classroom use.

Where in the United States?
Blackline Master 3

Common plants:

_____   _____

_____   _____

_____   _____

Common foods:

_____   _____

_____   _____

_____   _____

Children's games:

_____   _____

_____   _____

_____   _____

Unusual facts:

_____   _____

_____   _____

_____   _____

Copyright © SRA/McGraw-Hill. Permission is granted to reproduce this page for classroom use.

Project 5   Newscenter 3

Use after Lesson 103

TOPIC

Reading,

Writing,

Science, Math

Suggested Resources:

Blackline Masters 1 and 2; Research Assistant Software; local radio and television newscasts; interviews; magazines; newspapers; the Internet

Objective:

From bulletin boards, newspapers, and magazines to radio, television, and the Internet, there is always new information to read or hear about. Using a variety of resources, including videotapes of television news shows, study the parts of broadcast news. Use what you learn to develop your own newscast about school and community events and perform it for your class.

Suggested Activities:

Session One

Divide students into groups of at least four members each and pass out Blackline Master 1 to help describe the project to the students.

Have each group obtain a Project Startup form. The Project Startup form can be found on the Research Assistant Software. Each group should complete the Project Startup form with the required information and turn it in to the teacher.

Direct each group to obtain and complete a Tasks form from the Research Assistant Software.

Once tasks have been assigned, provide students with the location of other forms on the Research Assistant Software that might assist them in the organization of their individual tasks.

————————————— CHECKPOINT —————————————

Review the Project Startup form and Tasks form for each group; each student in the group should have an assignment.

Session Two

Allow time for students to use as many of the suggested resources as possible to complete the questions on Blackline Master 2. Encourage students to share information discovered with the class while reviewing the questions on the Blackline Master.

Possible answers for Blackline Master 2:
1. weather, local news, national news, sports, financial reports, human interest
2. Accept all reasonable answers. Possible answers are upcoming events, awards, and sports scores.
3. students, teachers, the principal

Direct each group to obtain and complete a Main Topic & Details form from the Research Assistant Software.

Conduct a class discussion to determine the time limit for each newscast.

———————————————— **CHECKPOINT** ————————————————

Review the Main Topic & Details form for each group to ensure that each group has begun to develop stories for the different parts of a newscast.

Session Three

Have each group obtain a copy of the Notes form found in the Research Assistant Software to organize its ideas. Direct students to the Sources form found in the Research Assistant Software. This form may also help them organize their information.

Students should continue to look for information to include in their presentations.

———————————————— **CHECKPOINT** ————————————————

Require groups to turn in their Notes forms with, at least, an outline of what their newscast will include. Check with individual students on their progress. Inform the class that a rough draft of each individual's presentation will be due at the beginning of the next project session.

Session Four

Rough drafts due. Meet with each group individually to review the rough draft. Allow time for editing and further class discussion if compromises need to be revisited.

Have each group obtain a Supplies Form found in the Research Assistant Software. The Supplies Form should be completed by the end of today's project time. Encourage students to share with you and other groups any supplies needed for their presentations.

Before the end of today's project time, ask each group to share with you any difficulties it may be experiencing regarding its presentation such as the amount of time that will be allowed for each segment of the news. If time allows, open the discussion to the entire class for classmates to offer additional help.

—————————————— **CHECKPOINT** ——————————————

At the end of today's project time, each group should have a majority of its presentation completed.

Session Five

Allow groups to have a dress rehearsal of the final newscast. Ask students to pay particular attention to length of the segments, their enunciation, speed of delivery, and the content. Students should make any needed changes prior to the final presentation.

Session Six

Presentation of the newscasts.

Evaluation/Answers:

Each presentation should be completed in the agreed amount of time. Individual students will be evaluated on the completion of their assigned task on the Task form.

Optional Discussion:

Have students complete the Self form from the Research Assistant Software. Facilitate a discussion in which the students discuss what they learned about themselves while working on the project, as well as their opinions regarding the difficulties they had completing their tasks.

Newscenter 3
Blackline Master 1

Objective:
From bulletin boards, newspapers, and magazines to radio, television, and the Internet, there is always new information to read or hear about. Using a variety of resources, including videotapes of television news shows, study the parts of broadcast news. Use what you learn to develop your own newscast about school and community events and perform it for your class.

Resource List:

☐ Research Assistant Software

☐ local radio and television newscasts

☐ interviews with students, teachers, parents, and local elected officials

☐ magazines

☐ newspapers

☐ the Internet

☐ _____

☐ _____

☐ _____

☐ _____

Copyright © SRA/McGraw-Hill. Permission is granted to reproduce this page for classroom use.

Newscenter 3

Blackline Master 2

1. List the main parts of a newscast:

    _____

    _____

    _____

2. What information do you think most of the students in your school would be interested in hearing about?

    _____

    _____

    _____

    _____

3. Who would have the information you seek?

    _____

    _____

    _____

    _____

Copyright © SRA/McGraw-Hill. Permission is granted to reproduce this page for classroom use.

Welcome to *SRA Research Assistant*

SRA Research Assistant provides students with the tools to take them through all the necessary steps to complete a research project.

By completing the series of forms in the *SRA Research Assistant*, students are better able to investigate their topic, organize facts, and prepare a cohesive, informative report.

SRA Research Assistant provides forms in four different areas:

- planning
- organizing
- presenting
- assessing

By using the forms available in each of these areas, students can be assured that their research will be well-documented from beginning to end. They will be able to show each stage of their project from the initial planning to the final self-assessment.

Starting *SRA Research Assistant*

No installation is needed. *SRA Research Assistant* runs from the CD-ROM.

Macintosh®

1. Insert the *SRA Research Assistant* CD-ROM into the CD-ROM drive. The disc window will open.
2. Double-click the *SRA Research Assistant* icon. After a brief introduction, the Project Selection screen will appear.

Windows® 95 and 98

1. Insert the *SRA Research Assistant* CD-ROM into the CD-ROM drive.
2. If the CD window doesn't open, double-click My Computer on the desktop then double-click SRA_RSCH.
3. Double-click SRA_RA.EXE.

   After a brief introduction, the Project Selection screen will appear.

Using *SRA Research Assistant*

The Project Selection Screen

The Project Selection screen is the first screen students will see as they begin working with *SRA Research Assistant*. From this screen, students can click on an existing project to work on or select "Add Project" in the Project pull-down menu and then key in the new project's name.

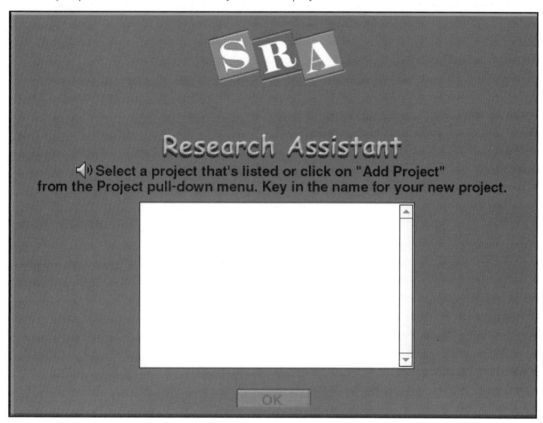

The Project Menu

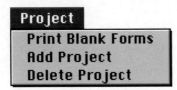

The Project pull-down menu provides students with the following options:

- "Print Blank Forms" allows you to print reproducible forms without a date or project data.
- "Add Project" allows students to create a new research project.
- "Delete Project" allows students to delete a research project and all the files associated with it.

The Edit Menu

The Edit pull-down menu provides students with the following commands, which can be used to edit forms:

- Undo
- Cut
- Copy
- Paste

The File Menu

File
Export Form for Word Processor
Print Form
Select Project
Quit   ⌘Q

The File pull-down menu provides students with the following options:

- "Export Form for Word Processor" allows students to save their work as text files.
- "Print Form" allows students to print the form on which they are working.
- "Select Project" allows students to return to the Project Selection screen.
- "Quit" allows students to close *SRA Research Assistant.*

Adding a Project

Each time students add a project, a folder is created that contains student work for that project. These folders are located in the *SRA Research Assistant* folder on the hard drive.

To add a project:

1. Students start *SRA Research Assistant* and wait for the Project Selection screen to appear.
2. Students select "Add Project" from the Project menu at the top of the screen. A text box appears.

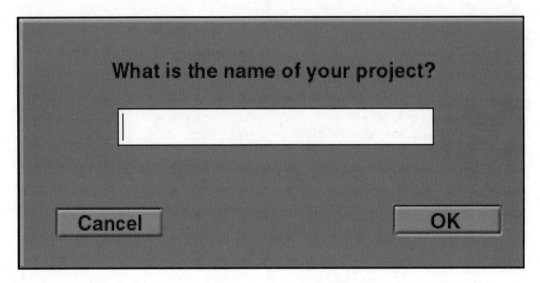

3. Students type the name of the project they want to add. Project names can have up to 30 characters.
4. Students will then click OK to return to the Project Selection screen.
5. The new project name will be highlighted. Click OK to open the first form and begin work on the project.

Opening a Project

1. From the Project Selection screen, students select the name of an existing project on which they want to work.
2. Students click OK to open the first form. Students may now work with any of the 18 forms provided by *SRA Research Assistant*.
3. Once students fill out forms, these forms will be saved to a folder named *SRA Research Assistant* on the hard drive.

   Please refer to the section of this guide entitled "The Forms" for detailed information on each one.

Deleting a Project

1. Students start *SRA Research Assistant* and wait for the Project Selection screen to appear.
2. Students select Delete Project from the Project menu at the top of the screen. A text box appears.
3. Students choose the name of the project they want to delete, then click OK.
4. Students will be asked again if they want to delete their project. If they do, they will click OK again and the project will be deleted.

Quitting *SRA Research Assistant*

1. Choose "Quit" from the File menu. The Credits screen will appear.
2. Click OK to return to the desktop.

The Forms

This section provides information on each of the 18 forms in *SRA Research Assistant*. Each form covers a different area of the research process and allows students the opportunity to use them all or to find those that best suit their particular research needs.

The forms are divided into four sections, each covering a specific aspect of the research process: planning, organizing, presenting, and assessing.

There is also a Glossary of terms the students may use while working on their projects.

 Tips

Each form has a light bulb in the upper right corner of the screen. This is the Tips button. Students can click this button for ideas to help them while working on each form. Tips vary from form to form, providing students with help specific to each one.

Saving Forms

SRA Research Assistant saves forms automatically as students work on them.

Project Startup

The Project Startup form asks students for basic facts about their project, including its title, description, and team members.

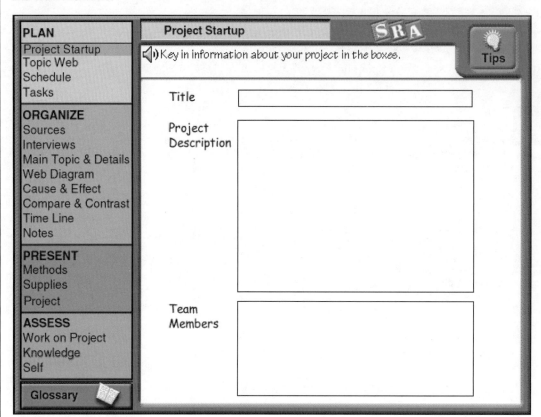

Topic Web

The Topic Web form helps students organize subtopics related to their main topic.

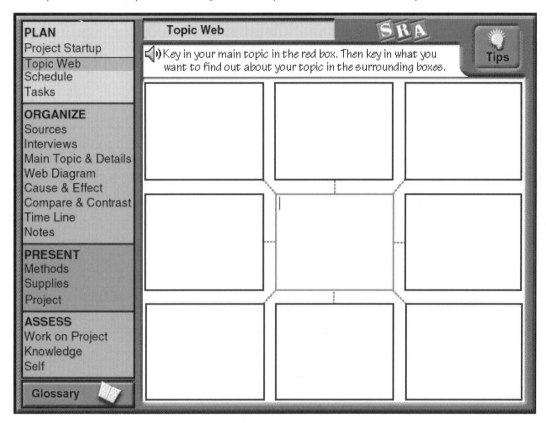

Schedule

The Schedule form provides a calendar for students to fill in with important dates related to their project.

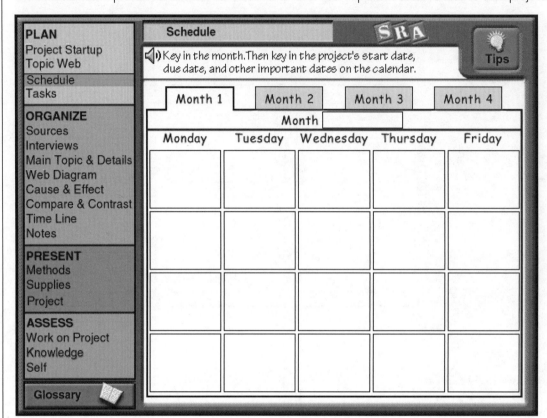

Tasks

The Tasks form gives students a place to assign tasks to members of their team.

PLAN	Tasks	SRA	Tips
PLAN Project Startup, Topic Web, Schedule			

PLAN
Project Startup
Topic Web
Schedule
Tasks

ORGANIZE
Sources
Interviews
Main Topic & Details
Web Diagram
Cause & Effect
Compare & Contrast
Time Line
Notes

PRESENT
Methods
Supplies
Project

ASSESS
Work on Project
Knowledge
Self

Glossary

◁))) List the tasks needed to be done for your project.
Key in the name of the team member who will do each task.

Tasks	Team Members

Sources

The Sources form is useful for recording the title, author, and other information about sources in which students found valuable information.

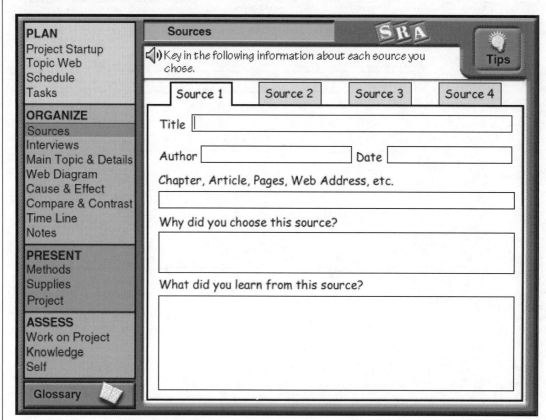

Interviews

The Interviews form allows students to record information about interviews they plan to conduct or have already conducted.

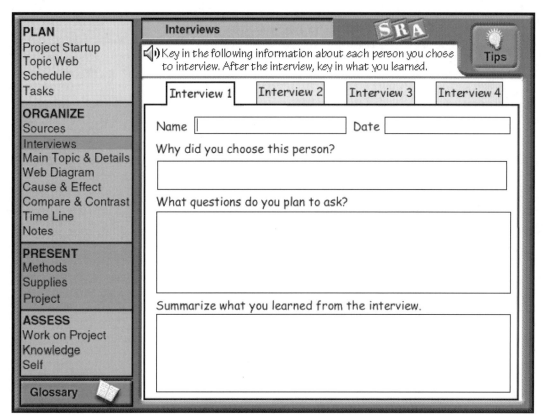

Main Topic & Details

The Main Topic & Details form helps students determine what is most important about the subject they are covering by giving them an area to list their project's main points.

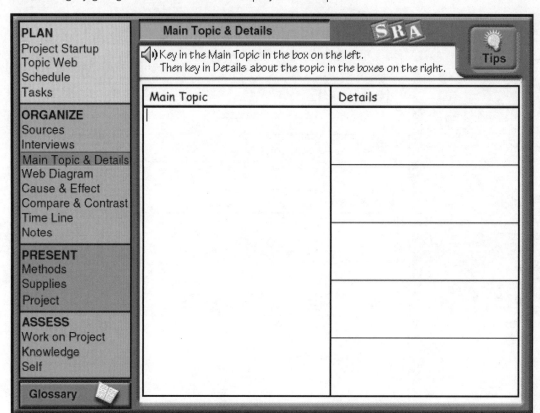

Web Diagram

Similar to the Topic Web form, the Web Diagram form provides students with the opportunity to organize subtopics by recording related information.

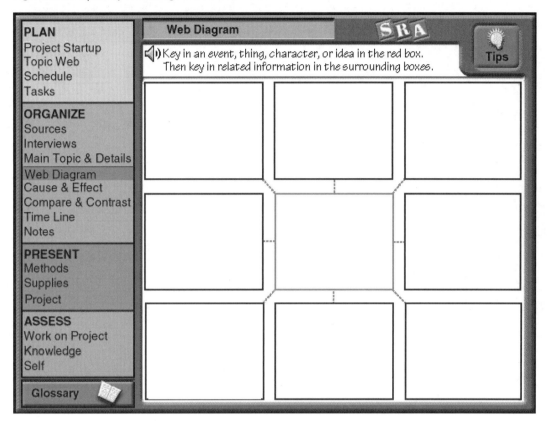

Cause & Effect

The Cause & Effect form is a place where students can record events and their effect on other occurrences.

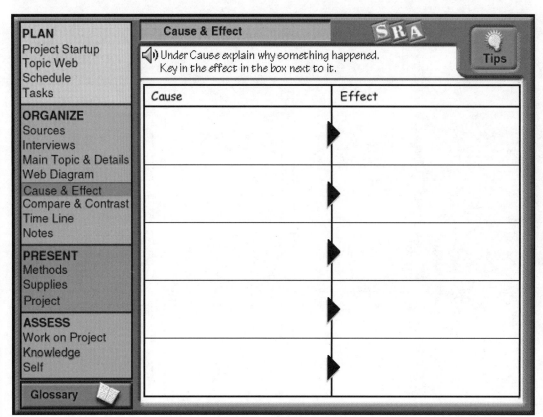

Compare & Contrast

The Compare & Contrast form provides students with a type of Venn diagram where they can record how things are different and how they are the same.

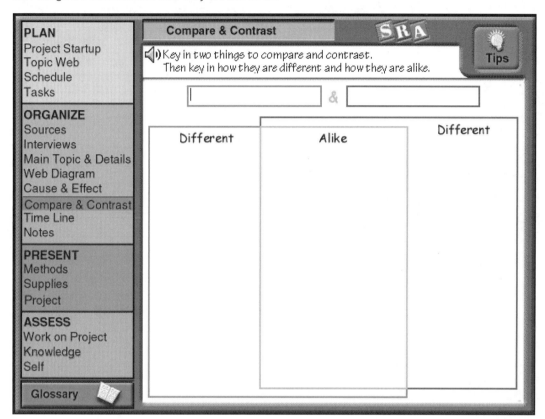

Time Line

The Time Line form provides students with an area to record events and the dates they occurred.

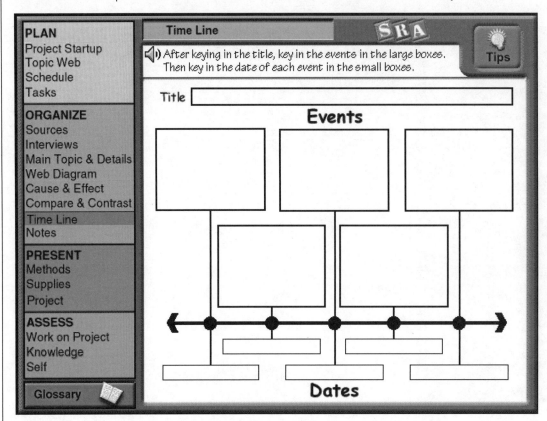

Notes

The Notes form provides an area to organize notes or to create an outline.

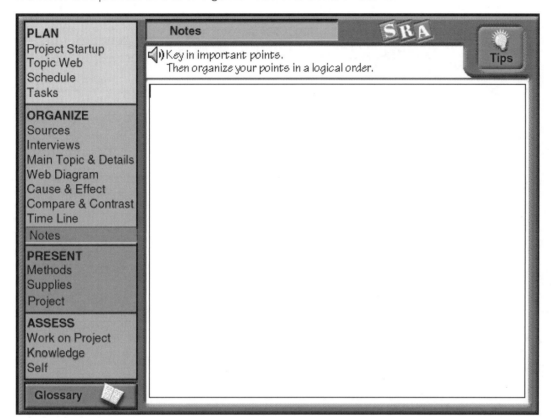

Methods

The Methods form asks students to consider the method(s) they would like to use when giving their presentation.

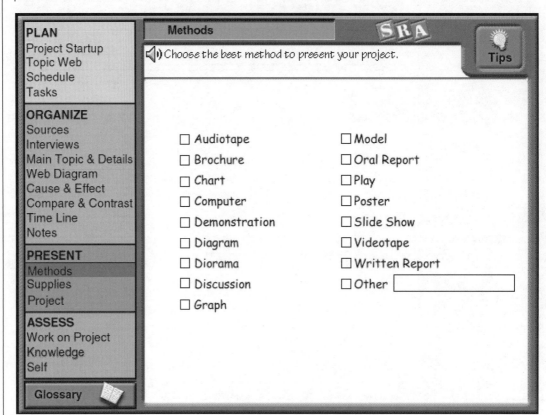

Supplies

The Supplies form asks students to consider supplies they will need based on their presentation method(s).

PLAN	Supplies	SRA

PLAN
Project Startup
Topic Web
Schedule
Tasks

ORGANIZE
Sources
Interviews
Main Topic & Details
Web Diagram
Cause & Effect
Compare & Contrast
Time Line
Notes

PRESENT
Methods
Supplies
Project

ASSESS
Work on Project
Knowledge
Self

Glossary

Supplies

◁)) Choose the supplies you may need to make and present your final project. Key in any supplies not listed.

Tips

Brochure Poster Written Report	Demonstration Discussion Oral Report Play	Audiotape Computer Slide Show Videotape	Diorama Model
☐ Computer	☐ Costumes	☐ Audio Recorder	☐ Box
☐ Copy Machine	☐ Notes	☐ Audiotape	☐ Clay
☐ Crayons	☐ Outline	☐ Batteries	☐ Cloth
☐ Glue	☐ Props	☐ Computer	☐ Colored Paper
☐ Magic Marker	☐ Scenery	☐ Extension Cord	☐ Crayons
☐ Paint	☐ Script	☐ Microphone	☐ Glue
☐ Paper		☐ Projector	☐ Markers
☐ Pictures		☐ Screen	☐ Paint
☐ Poster Board		☐ Software	☐ Papier-mâché
☐ Report Cover		☐ Transparencies	☐ Pencils
		☐ VCR	☐ Wire
		☐ Video Camera	
		☐ Videotape	

Other Supplies

Project

The Project form gives students an area to key in an oral report, written report, or other information.

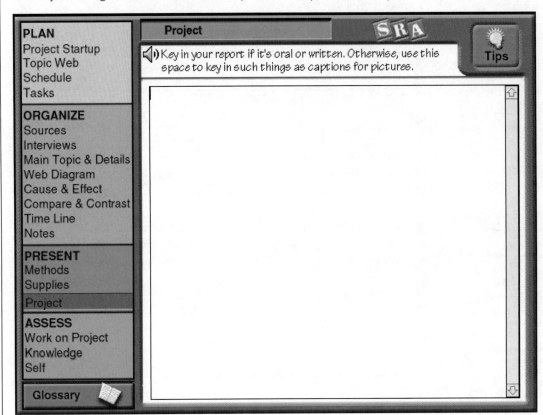

Work on Project

The Work on Project form provides students with the opportunity to reflect on the work they did on their project.

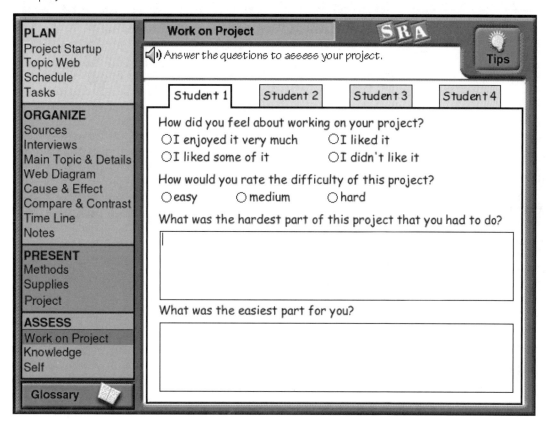

Knowledge

The Knowledge form asks students to consider the topics they chose now that their research is done.

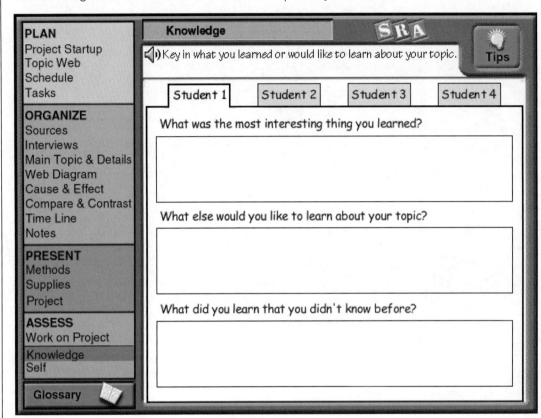

Self

The Self form asks students to consider what they learned about themselves during this project.

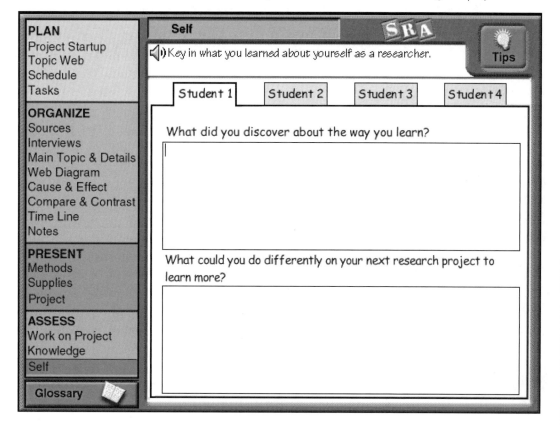

Glossary

The *SRA Research Assistant* also provides students with a Glossary containing definitions of words they might find in *SRA Research Assistant* and in their independent research.

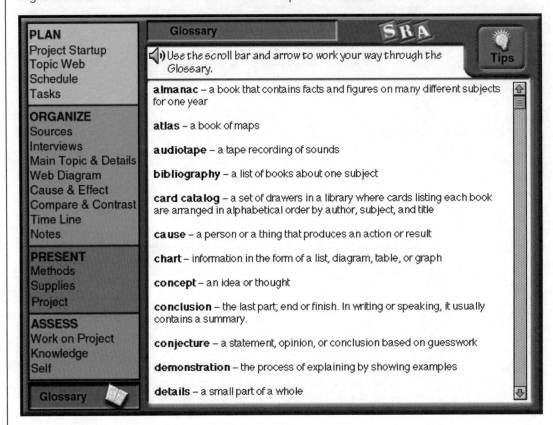

The screen shows a glossary interface. On the left navigation panel:

PLAN
Project Startup
Topic Web
Schedule
Tasks

ORGANIZE
Sources
Interviews
Main Topic & Details
Web Diagram
Cause & Effect
Compare & Contrast
Time Line
Notes

PRESENT
Methods
Supplies
Project

ASSESS
Work on Project
Knowledge
Self

Glossary

The main panel titled "Glossary":

Use the scroll bar and arrow to work your way through the Glossary.

almanac – a book that contains facts and figures on many different subjects for one year

atlas – a book of maps

audiotape – a tape recording of sounds

bibliography – a list of books about one subject

card catalog – a set of drawers in a library where cards listing each book are arranged in alphabetical order by author, subject, and title

cause – a person or a thing that produces an action or result

chart – information in the form of a list, diagram, table, or graph

concept – an idea or thought

conclusion – the last part; end or finish. In writing or speaking, it usually contains a summary.

conjecture – a statement, opinion, or conclusion based on guesswork

demonstration – the process of explaining by showing examples

details – a small part of a whole